Boats and Ships

Contents

written by Pam Holden

Boats are used for work or for fun. A boat that goes by a sail in the wind is a sailboat.

Sometimes people have a race
to see who can go fast.
The wind pushes on the sail
to make it go.

A boat with a motor and
a cabin is a motorboat.
Some people call it a launch.

They can go to new
places to have a holiday.
They can sleep in the
cabin in bunks.

A big boat that goes across
the sea is a ship.
Ships are used for work.

Some big ships take people a long way for a holiday. They are called cruise ships.

cruise ship

Some ships take big things
across the world.
They are called cargo ships.

They can take things like
cars and animals!
Some things go in big
boxes on container ships.

A boat that goes under the
water is a submarine.
It can find things that are
lost down in the deep sea.
10

People can go down in a submarine
to see what it is like there.
They see lots of fish and plants.

submarine

Sometimes boats go to find people who need help.
They are called rescue boats.

They can give people a ride home.
Sometimes they pull boats that can't go.

Fishing boats go out to
sea to get a lot of fish.
They take the fish back for
people in the town to eat.
NOORDSTER
WR-3

Some people use small boats
to go and get their fish.
They don't go out a long way.

15

A boat that people have for their home is a houseboat. They live there all the time!